Peacock Luggage

MONIZA ALVI

Peacock Luggage

PETER DANIELS

Smith/Doorstop Books

Published 1992 by
Smith/Doorstop Books
The Poetry Business
51 Byram ArcAde
Westgate
Huddersfield HD1 1ND

Copyright © The Authors 1992
All rights reserved

ISBN 1 869961 33 1

Typeset at The Poetry Business
Printed by Victoria Press, Holmfirth
Distributors: Password (Books) Ltd., 23 New Mount Street, Manchester
M4 4DE

The Poetry Business gratefully acknowledges the help of Kirklees
Metropolitan Council and Yorkshire & Humberside Arts.

ERRATA

p15, line12
"In the square there are those who beg"
p25, line9
"Mary Jo knows, tells me she's been looking"
p25, line18
"bleaches the morning to the bone."

CONTENTS

Moniza Alvi

Indian Cooking 9
Presents from my Aunts in Pakistan 10
Arrival 1946 12
Luckbir 13
The Country at my Shoulder 14
The Sari 16
Hill 17
I Make Pencil Drawings, Scribbles, Bales of Hay 18
The Afterworld 19
Afternoon at the Cinema 20
Neighbourhood 21
Pilgrimage 22
Housebreaker 23
I Would Like to be a Dot in a Painting by Miro 24
Meeting an ex-Pupil on a Spring Morning 25
I Was Raised in a Glove Compartment 26
On Finding a Letter to Mrs Vickers 27

Peter Daniels

Ancestors 31
A Video of my Father 32
The Dark Piano 33
Portions 34
Sculpture 36
A Demon Explains 37
Excesses of the Prior of Inchcolm 38
Navigation 39
The Large Garden 40
Kentish Town 41
Hampstead in June 42
Royal Wedding 46
An Eclipse 47
Pastoral Interlude 48
Homecoming 49
Seminar for Nomads 50

MONIZA ALVI

The Country at my Shoulder

INDIAN COOKING

The bottom of the pan was a palette —
paprika, cayenne, dhania,
haldi, heaped like powder-paints.

Melted ghee made lakes, golden rivers.
The keema frying, my mother waited
for the fat to bubble to the surface.

Friends brought silver-leaf.
I dropped it on khir —
special rice pudding for parties.

I tasted the landscape, customs
of my father's country —
its fever on biting a chilli.

PRESENTS FROM MY AUNTS IN PAKISTAN

They sent me a salwar kameez
  peacock-blue,
    and another,
glistening like an orange split open,
  embossed slippers, gold and black
    points curling.
Candy-striped glass bangles
snapped, drew blood.
  Like at school, fashions changed
    in Pakistan —
the salwar bottoms were broad and stiff,
    then narrow.
My aunts chose an apple-green sari,
  silver-bordered
    for my teens.

I tried each satin-silken top —
  was alien in the sitting-room.
I could never be as lovely
    as those clothes — I longed
for denim and corduroy.
  My costume clung to me
    and I was aflame,
I couldn't rise up out of its fire,
  half-English,
    unlike Aunt Jamila.

I wanted my parents' camel-skin lamp —
  switching it on in my bedroom,
to consider the cruelty
    and the transformation
from camel to shade,
  marvel at the colours
    like stained-glass.
My mother cherished her jewellery —

Indian gold, dangling, filigree.
But it was stolen from our car.
The presents were radiant in my wardrobe.
My aunts requested cardigans
from Marks and Spencers.

My salwar kameez
didn't impress the schoolfriend
who sat on my bed, asked to see
my weekend clothes.
But often I admired the mirror-work,
tried to glimpse myself
in the miniature glass circles,
recall the story —
how the three of us
sailed to England.
Prickly heat had me screaming on the way.
I ended up in a cot
in my English grandmother's dining-room,
found myself alone,
playing with a tin boat.

I pictured my birthplace
from fifties' photographs.
When I was older
there was conflict, a fractured land
throbbing through newsprint.
Sometimes I saw Lahore —
my aunts in shaded rooms,
screened from male visitors,
sorting presents,
wrapping them in tissue.

Or there were beggars, sweeper-girls
and I was there —
of no fixed nationality,
staring through fretwork
at the Shalimar Gardens.

ARRIVAL 1946

The boat docked in at Liverpool.
From the train Tariq stared
at an unbroken line of washing
from the North West to Euston.

These are strange people, he thought —
an Empire, and all this washing,
the underwear, the Englishman's garden.

It was Monday, and very sharp.

LUCKBIR

My aunt Luckbir had full red lips,
sari borders broad like silver cities,
gold flock wallpaper in her sitting room.
Purple curtains opened

on a small, square garden
where Uncle Anwar fed the birds
and photographed Aunt, her costume
draped over a kitchen stool,

the backdrop — a garden fence and roses.
Luckbir found her Cardiff neighbours
very kind — thanked them in a letter
to *Woman's Own,*

spoke to me warmly of Jane Austen
remembered from an overseas degree.
Aunt had no wish to go out, take a job,
an evening class.

Picking at rice on pyrex
she grew thin — thinner.
In my dreams she was robust,
had a Western hairstyle, stepped outside.

After she died young
Uncle tried everything —
astronomy, yoga, cookery.
His giant TV set flickers into life —

a video of the ice-skating championship.
Has he kept Aunt's clothes,
let their shimmer slip through his hands?

THE COUNTRY AT MY SHOULDER

There's a country at my shoulder,
growing larger — soon it will burst,
rivers will spill out, run down my chest.

My cousin Azam wants visitors to play
ludo with him all the time.
He learns English in a class of seventy.

And I must stand to attention
with the country at my shoulder.
There's an execution in the square —

The women's dupattas are wet with tears.
The offices have closed
for the white-hot afternoon.

But the women stone-breakers chip away
at boulders, dirt on their bright hems.
They await the men and the trucks.

I try to shake the dust from the country,
smooth it with my hands.
I watch Indian films —

Everyone is very unhappy,
or very happy,
dancing garlanded through parks.

I hear of bribery, family quarrels,
travellers' tales — the stars
are so low you think you can touch them.

Moniza Alvi

Uncle Aqbar drives down the mountain
to arrange his daughter's marriage.
She's studying Christina Rossetti.

When the country bursts, we'll meet.
Uncle Kamil shot a tiger,
it hung over the wardrobe, its jaws

fixed in a roar — I wanted to hide
its head in a towel.
The country has become my body —

I can't break bits off.
The men go home in loose cotton clothes.
In the square are those who beg —

And those who beg for mercy.
Azam passes the sweetshop,
names the sugar monuments Taj Mahal.

I water the country with English rain,
cover it with English words.
Soon it will burst, or fall like a meteor.

THE SARI

Inside my mother
I peered through a glass porthole.
The world beyond was hot and brown.

They were all looking in on me —
Father, Grandmother,
the cook's boy, the sweeper-girl,
the bullock with the sharp
shoulderblades,
the local politicians.

My English grandmother
took a telescope
and gazed, across continents.

All the people unravelled a sari.
It stretched from Lahore to Hyderabad,
wavered across the Arabian Sea,
shot through with stars,
fluttering with sparrows and quails.
They threaded it with roads,
undulations of land.

Eventually
they wrapped and wrapped me in it
whispering 'Your body is your country'.

HILL

The hill heaps up her darknesses.

It is too cold for me to reach
the top. Yet she is always supreme,

dropping the lakes to her feet
and brushing them with her full skirt.

She'll never stoop down to her domain
now she has the luxury of a view.

In charge of greys and green-greys
she structures the late afternoon

with inky threads from stalling kites
and the hurtlings of solo footballers.

Slowly, she discards all detail —
offers me her dissolving horizons.

I MAKE PENCIL DRAWINGS, SCRIBBLES, BALES OF HAY

I make pencil drawings, scribbles, bales of hay,
bundles of twigs, a bonfire with parts torn out,
rough shapes of a man leaning on a woman

who leans on a child.

The distance is a simple line they turn to,
a tangle of rosebushes, the signature
of a dead queen — all black loops and angles.

Moniza Alvi

THE AFTERWORLD

When your parents are gone
you will wear a white dress
and lock yourself inside
their empty house.

Daily, you'll pace the hollow boards
to the door, where you think you see
your father,
and the tree behind you
will be tapping greenly at the window.

A thousand times you'll write
at a child's desk
versions of the stories
they still pass to you in fragments.

Across them spreads your long hair —
it is still golden.
But you will not own anything
except the sudden sunlight
shining through your parents' hallway
up into your bedroom.

AFTERNOON AT THE CINEMA

You are watching a film you can't understand
with the man you once lived with
who reassures you that he can't understand it either
but he supposes it's not supposed to be exactly —
What was the word he used?

The film — you've seen it before —
it was a mystery then, and now you've missed
the sheet with interpretations on it.
Perhaps you'll get one later at the door.
The screen pours out its pictures
mirrors swaying like water
mirrors shivering in fragments
to walk through, turn back through
while pairs of lovers interchange and
there are murders and crowds and everyone
is tumbling off the screen.

You are watching a film you can't understand
with the man you once lived with.
You're in flames and falling on a mirror.
Was that something that he said?

NEIGHBOURHOOD

Next door they were always fighting
calling each other Mr and Mrs
the names barking away
at the back of our chimney.

There were families with bitten
trickles of children
who pushed prams full of babies
junk and little dogs, smothered
and dressed in baby clothes.

On the run from my family troubles
I'd sneak to a back corner
of the playing field to savour
a terrible garden through the fence
where empty petfood cans were traps
in the Amazon grass.

And once Jim Skerry
bruised with dirt, never at school
came out through the din
behind his back door
wearing a hard brown plastic wig.
He sauntered off to the street.

PILGRIMAGE

On that dreamy late afternoon
the bushes alive with cabbage whites
Tom led me down the tangled pathway
between the mysteries of back gardens
and the top of the railway bank
where we were not supposed to play.

At last he pointed out a clearing
a sandy dip in the bank
and there it lay
a long fat turd.
It was Neil, Tom said.
Neil did it.
Other children had arived
so we all gathered round
in a wide circle to study it
and it seemed to stare at us
burnished rich brown
almost kingly
as if the sun enjoyed it too —
an offering from a pale quiet boy.
Not one of us was disappointed.

Someone tried to burn it.
One by one we clambered up the bank
and trekked along the pathway.
Then later, at the tea-table
I thought of what Neil had left
in the vanishing sunlight.

HOUSEBREAKER

I dash my fist against the white walls —
they dent coldly like ice-cream.
Smug as a conjuror in the quiet hallway,
my face grazes slightly in the light.
Busy in the bedroom, I'm spell-blinding,
cupping nightmares in my hands,
turning them into silk scarves.
I long to feel the charred paper breath
of sleepers rising and falling on my skin.
If they wake, I'll loom up in monochrome,
I'll tell them how to catch a rat —
dye an ear of barley blue, for bait.

Moonlight whitens the lawn. A drained
swimming pool. Car on the track.

Is that a guitar in the corner of the room?
I could tell them how the lute is played differently.
Downstairs I'm a strange bird in a classical setting.
I fly into china, make cool, surgical music,
slide on the rugs, skating for information.

The house I gut goes down like a ship in the night,
At dawn, like a conspiracy, it rises behind my back.

I WOULD LIKE TO BE A DOT
IN A PAINTING BY MIRO

I would like to be a dot in a painting by Miro.

Barely distinguishable from other dots,
it's true, but quite uniquely placed.
And from my dark centre

I'd survey the beauty of the linescape
and wonder — would it be worthwhile
to roll myself towards the lemon stripe,

Centrally poised, and push my curves
against its edge, to get myself
a little extra attention?

But it's fine where I am.
I'll never make out what's going on
around me, and that's the joy of it.

The fact that I'm not a perfect circle
makes me more interesting in this world.
People will stare forever —

Even the most unemotional get excited.
So here I am, on the edge of animation,
a dream, a dance, a fantastic construction,

A child's adventure.
And nothing in this tawny sky
can get too close, or move too far away.

MEETING AN EX-PUPIL ON A
SPRING MORNING

Mary Jo, schoolgirl turned dental nurse
is smiling outside the surgery.
The wind clears the sky over Southwark Park.
In the sun-whitened street Mary Jo smiles —
a man in a poplar tree lops off branches,
leaves shine like silver on the fence.

Mary Jo smiles as if composing herself
for a photograph. This used to be my dentist.
Mary Jo knows, tells us she's been looking
at my records. And then she smiles.
I see x-rays of my teeth blown up cinematic
on hoardings all over Bermondsey.

The blossoming trees brush against them
and hurl their petals to the ground
like sweetpapers. Mary Jo smiles.
A passing woman fills her baby's bottle
with Pepsi. And the sun, like flash-light
bleaches the morning to bone.

I WAS RAISED IN A GLOVE COMPARTMENT

I was raised in a glove compartment.
The gloves held out limp fingers —

in the dark I touched them.
I bumped against the First Aid tin,

and rolled on notepads and maps.
I never saw my mother's face —

sometimes
her gloved hand would reach for me.

I existed in the quiet — I listened
for the sound of the engine.

ON FINDING A LETTER TO MRS VICKERS ON THE PENNINE WAY

A bird with a torn tail hops under ferns
and points its beak to the wall.

A letter to Mrs Vickers is trodden into the path —
colours have run into edges soft as cotton.

Mrs Vickers, Mrs Vickers
you have won, you have almost won
a Ford Escort. We of the Prizes Department
are sending you a draft of the Award Certificate.

Earth trickles over it like a child's pattern.

Mrs Vickers, calling your number at Stoneway
we would like to tell you
you're in with a winning chance.
Don't miss the cellophane window.

It shines like a dirty film of ice.

Mrs Vickers, don't forget to tell us
all about yourself.
Then tread this well into the path
where the mossy fronds dart like fishes —

And the bird fans out its broken tail.

PETER DANIELS

Seminar for Nomads

ANCESTORS

I am from sand and clay, or wind and foam.
Add me and multiply me every day,
follow the trail of crumbs till you come home.

Finger the names that every leather tome
scripted and scratched, and see if they can say
I am from sand and clay, or wind and foam.

Catching a gale force nine at the aerodrome,
Grandmother's broom eloped with Santa's sleigh:
follow the trail of crumbs till you come home.

Touched by a mermaid with a pearly comb,
Grandfather's muddy footprints made him stay:
I am from sand and clay, or wind and foam.

Meeting and parting with each chromosome,
shaking the bag they shared their DNA:
follow the trail of crumbs till you come home.

I am a gasping fish, a grinning gnome,
I have a bone to pick, a tune to play,
I am from sand and clay, or wind and foam:
follow the trail of crumbs till you come home.

A VIDEO OF MY FATHER

At ease among statisticians, he settles into his chair
to trace back his subject for the archives.
His developing concepts arise, like The Advancing Wave
in a Spatial Birth Process. My nonsense-mind is
daydreaming probabilities, how I am where I am.

Telling of southward-moving mathematicals, 'We
Scots . . . ' he remarks; taking me aback, though he keeps on
a few Scots consonants. Always he is fondest of Leeds:
his first job, the Wool Research Board, drawing out
meanings from thousands of snapped-off ends of yarn.

London-Jewish baby, carried back north to where
Grandmother's herring boat came in. Families don't
add up. Look for some balancing factors: at the piano,
grasping the precision of Chopin; learning from a neighbour
the reconstruction of a watch, counterpoint of ratios.

At home, interpreting Grandmother's cabbage soup, her
Yiddish-Russian, her mental arithmetic. Bar-Mitzvah:
God's rules to measure the arbitrary lives, the walk
from synagogue to tenement door. Desire for the true
parameters, from the simple Standard Deviation, to

The Maximum of a Random Walk. But where I have walked
is not his Edinburgh: this window, years after his mother
nailed it up. From her time, I have one early memory: the lace,
the teacups, Arthur's seat, railings at Portobello. No Scot,
no Jew, it's not mine: except the remainder, recurring.

THE DARK PIANO

In this song, there's the old piano smell. It's a
bitter-chocolate varnish, with dust from the felt inside
lightening the hard and solid with a peppery tone.

Engineered into the steel frame is the fiction that
the strings are asleep under the frontage, while
they are all stretched, working harder than the finger
writing facts with a touch. The way some people speak.

Shut the lid: pianos happen in the dark. Once
as a child I awoke at night, positive there was an
arpeggio going on downstairs.

Was this a loud secret of my father's, putting
music about the house, as a release? For his
tune, or for the instrument? My ears or my mind?
Concentrate, practise, and play it for me.

And in this song there's a voice that draws up
a soft performance where I hear that smell.

PORTIONS

Prettiness looks like
how the things I'm fond of
organise themselves for me to view them.
The bodies and landscapes
enter my perspective
measured to my frame.

Every day I need
to borrow some pain:
for instance I will consume a fraction
of whatever leaps the dark gap
from the wide screen
to the seats in front.

Otherwise things unsteady
me to create my heart,
and life does harm, as love explains,
to spoil the face of pure meaning.
Go pleading for pictures
where beauty can argue back.

I have bribed my senses
to sing me to friendly danger;
I want to chase the great bear
who can protect with my fear;
I will make love defending my own portion,
helpless till somebody faces me, and I relent.

I stick his face in my head,
clip a sketch to the easel.
While I work on the portrait
I pick a tune for the headphones,
which the voice enclosed can spell out
in the secret alphabet fingered by songs.

SCULPTURE

I balance a few nuances before
tackling major structural problems.
Adjust a few details, a perfectly
turned mouth, a heroic plume.
Never mind that they fall over.
At this stage I am not concerned
to strengthen the knees, or check
the quality of stone. A few
girders or a concrete fill-in later
can hold up any defects, and
used with style can look impressively
casual. I gather up waste aluminium
and plastic sheets, to hide what
can't be mended: then catch onto
the pure dream, and hold my breath
for the moment ot its
pedestalization.

A DEMON EXPLAINS

I don't interrupt what you ask — the more
you want, the simpler the message. You see
how perfect the world is, it's a doddle
if you don't have to hold up both its ends.

Some of the shames and agonies haven't even been
invented yet, but that doesn't matter. You can
find enough sin in this week's local paper
to suit anybody's whole damnation.

The lowest bitterness and pain when they
attacked your own self is more than revenged
when I answer for you, make you burn something,
chop down a symbol because, well . . . it was meaningless.

Whether that cloud is incense or smoke,
underneath is always a fire. It only needs
one indefinite article to ignite a lie,
if that's what you want from me.

EXCESSES OF THE PRIOR
OF INCHCOLM

deposed from office, 1224

A monk is illuminating
aspects of the deadlier sins.
The Prior is much in his mind.
The blue snake twined
round the capital of Pride
follows his long smooth shape.
Something of his in the smirk
of the Scarlet Whore.

The Prior does not inspect the work.
He strides freely, he is not afraid
of the hellfires they resentfully
score down for him. Along this road
he will elevate self and soul: to see
his priority shining out beyond
the stony shape of the cloistered island.

NAVIGATION

Having to navigate kyles and islands
of tact and tokenism, look how we use
these old instruments, ornamented, blunt,
possessed with their own wilful logic.
We know how to read them because of
our own crazy spellings, the gift of twists
grown in, our compensated injuries
from the extremity of your whirlpool,
the wrenching jaws of the many heads
of my English assumptions.
Probably we're glad not knowing too precisely
how to go on through.

THE LARGE GARDEN

The Large Garden is a plain island
hidden in the obvious, a long open
arm of the Atlantic: not hard to place
but hard to reach, for gaps in timetables
that sail for more remarkable landings.

Clouds mask the mountains on each side,
and drift off them, hanging with rainbows.
This flatter piece is overlooked, aground
in its loch. No beaches but the barnacle shelves.
Children do their best with winkle crevices.

Home from Glasgow to stay now, she teaches
a language to its own people. We are in
her daughter's cottage — 'A house in use means
another light. Winter, it's empty - come and see
the moon shine clear onto the frosty mountains.'

This house is not empty for its own pleasure,
nor to create more room for other holidays.
This hospitality may come from rules of
honour extending into tourist business,
but to be visited is not to be at home.

And from this long space where we are
handfuls of strangers come to be curious, I
go back to London, where my own belonging,
my home at random in so many, is hidden in
the great, the spoilt, the visited, the obvious.

Peter Daniels

KENTISH TOWN

Along a row of tall alcoves in retaining
walls of dark brick, the platform ranges
classical as a plinth, sweeping the curve.

The grandeur of travel. Ostentatiously
she spreads her fur coat over a station
bench, and positions two suitcases beyond
easy reach. The empty length of the station
so luxurious, the space is hers, inconvenience
a privilege. Sunshine is absorbed by the charred
railway wall, as on a few hundred Saturdays
before this one: its warmth especially for her.

'When's the next train?' she asks me. I am there
to appreciate the beauty of the question. 'Where
does it go?' I tell her: Moorgate. 'Well, I think I'm
going to Ramsgate.' Spoken as if I was misled,
being tactful. She leads her dog on an
elliptical parade before she settles on
another bench: just as the train itself
enters. Fast, comfortable, nearly empty,
nearly at the end of the line. Safe. Time
to recollect herself and her belongings,
and step into the carriage she has chosen.

HAMPSTEAD IN JUNE

Circumstances: teatime at Kenwood; the weather
is hot at last; and because today is the Queen's
Official Birthday, the orchestra is giving
an especially cultured version of the Anthem.

The crowd is spread out about right to be poised
satisfactorily around the tables; we can use
so much experience each. All over the Heath
we manage to create our special clumps
and communities. Here in the gardens we cluster
in some very ordinary and some fairly
untypical sets. People in love with
various ice creams jostle to get their
life stories told, mark out their places.

Certain types. There are cautious and unstylish
men, one of them capped with a knotted
handkerchief against the heat, and women who
take their cardigans as veils, like makeshift nuns.
Away from the more intimate bushes, a few
odd-numbered groups of bearded gay men are
conversationally tuning themselves to
each other. And at a nearby table are these
elderly Jewish couples, establishing their own
tea-table style. The man in shirtsleeves
has a star tattoo on his arm.

The pigeons are ready, everywhere
they land on unattended food, some even on
plates in use. People offer crumbs to the
sparrows, which are not so big and beady-eyed.
Nature is prepared to mingle with us.

The Heath has folded open in a warm breeze
accommodating parts of London into a
huge green street crossed over with more
population, more poodles, than the land
wants to specify. Bushes survive from when
this was all the wild outskirts. The same
woodlands have been pictured in oils: with a
small Gipsy camp in one corner, gaily painted but
without figures, a single twist of smoke
implying life. These days, further outwards
any North Circular direction is not far to
the fancy-brick suburbs. Jehovah's
Witnesses will be trying the doorchimes
but no-one is in this afternoon.

Up on Parliament Hill, displaying
all the anchored ambitions, the kites float
and tumble: London stays where it is for now.
Deep in his nonchalance, a teenager
skates by, carrying the style and fashion shade
of the cashmere he wears like a prayer shawl.

Down the slope and around the panorama, musters
that semi-uncharted city, full of everybody's
characteristics, where some homosexuals
are also Jews, and so on: a congregation
of the badges people grow up with, or find, or
are given. Riches to tabulate in the human
landscape, the colours of stars and shapes for
someone to create a decorative map of symbols on
stratifications. And so much to do, for someone
who can find the motivating data to police
their standards of identity, to push them on
to the end, and to the very end.

After the getting through, salvaged alive and
human, he joined the tea-companions in a luckier
city: the star remains etched in his skin.
Awkwardly, onlookers like me can feel a
prestige of suffering he wears, and I
speculate about its privilege. Kenwood is not
his Vienna: but happy, today. These cakes are
stale, but we enjoy them, our circumstances.
The distinctions exist and are cultivated: people
being, doing, making the causes of hatred — simple
equations, unnameables that do not
carry logic. Nobody is making precise
arguments on politics and crime worth
one destroyed person, or a million.

And the star also contains its own meanings from
long before. Black skin means more than the
centuries of slavery. Love and sex are still
more than the way an unknowing virus can
change hands. And in the meanwhile
regeneration has to ask better than to walk
ignorant in sunshine. Information,
death's classified statistics; experience of
the victim's clownish unpopularity; truth against
the new blood libels; and some strength to imagine
the Gestapo now in Flask Walk, where a man
is hounded down that Amsterdam street, or to see
at Highgate Ponds the heaped bodies of Babi Yar.

We get ready for an ordinary summer of
falling in love, learning lessons, and providing
fire extinguishers. We raise our kites and banners
in the open-ended fresh air.
On a street in
Germany an elderly Jehovah's Witness is still
holding out the Watch Tower.
On this hill
A Black family cheer their bird-shaped
African flag, that stands trembling
on a string above the dome of grass.

ROYAL WEDDING

It takes precision to project
all the responsibilities:
the chamberlains and equerries
have organised the footprints
to exploit the fullest joy
from every stiff bishop, duke in furs
or spouse-of-head-of-state.

What magic! What holy matrimonious power!
The organ spreads its gluey warmth to seal
their vows. The hopeful glow from haloes,
and camera lighting, will protect their bedpost.

Meanwhile, two of us were on a train:
luminaries in our own procession,
going home
without a licence.

Peter Daniels 47

AN ECLIPSE

When we were getting in the way of the moon
I waited up for the shadow, but the moon in my window
lost me behind branches. Out in the street, the sky
had still not hidden it, at nearly four a.m. I went to bed
but never slept: I had to take the next day off.

You told me later how, during your night shift,
you took the chance to climb the hospital stairwell, up
and around the slow-breathing building, above
a dead city, angling floor by floor to keep
the sliding discs of dark and light in view.

48   Peter Daniels

PASTORAL INTERLUDE

For two years now, my allergic throat has been roughening drily
under each warm wind full of pollen as a gardener's paintbrush.
Some cells in me are ready to fight against it, some others
are impressed by suggestions of progress from spring to summer.

Over this time, some changes of atmosphere. I could love
the sweet ways of your dukedom as I love flowers, not too close.
Now, I walk my mile home from you, past the park. The dry screams
are the peacocks roosting. The moon is glowing from two years ago.

         *   *   *   *   *   *   *

'Be the late one for once, get away, keep walking,' — a message
from some unreliable hormone climbing me up that hill, alone
and free: an illusion, another city fiction. The place was even
a kind of home, one of our own places. Escape was unconvincing.

And I began to notice: breathing the open breeze took in
a drag of discomfort, crowding my cells. Though it surprised me
how those flowers you brought would hurt me, I could never
imagine saying 'enough', to be cool and empty, satisfied.

Crossing the open spaces and woods, meeting a few aimlessly
purposeful people, I was taking my brief exile briskly through
this particular forest. Flowers opened their throats, welcoming,
unwelcome. All the soothing ice-creams had been shut away.

By now the wind was brushing harder for nightfall, dusting London
with invisible gold agony. I was walking away from a sunset,
a quick impressionistic row of smudges, up the hill towards
London's orange glow, and the orange moon huge over St Paul's.

HOMECOMING

History has been going on as if we made our home in it.
There may be only twenty ways to twist its usual tune:
you can't listen to more than half. You follow them, until
the struggle to get home will make you want to fast-forward,
put your thoughts into birdsong, but the birds are croaking.

The children are craning for a good look; there are rumours
of a right way to draw peacocks; later at home they will
invent and explain, as they can in their own half of life, until
it has tipped suddenly into the other. How time accelerates:
express each moment as a fraction of your life so far.

I still work as if dedication brought reward, a place to rest,
which may be only somewhere for our stiffening bodies.
Trudging the old road, I think of new ways home, until
it feels like somewhere else: home is invented, a fiction,
a lie. On the way, moments to enjoy, rehearsals to endure.

Once we feared the forest might eat us all up, but we've been
hacking through it to produce free will, by processes
committing us to maintenance for half infinity: until
our own faith destroys what it believed in, and we can't
come home, chuck off our old tired shoes, and scream.

SEMINAR FOR NOMADS

On the Common, they've cleared it all away:
the props from the mad party, the giant cups
upturned, stowed inwards on the long truck.
All ready to go, to unpack again later.

In the studio the block still stands
where the sculptor left it. The very tools
not put away, not abandoned: kept out,
ready to come in useful sometime.

In the empty city they are pitching camp
and waiting, among the streaky concrete
monuments to traffic. You found the track,
but you might not be lucky with a train.

In the lab, the task is cloning the mammoth:
because it isn't there, but it should be, might be
a miracle out of holy relics, a saint from a toenail.
It may be no good, but we don't know that yet.

In the booth, they have come to a formula.
Harry the Happy Paranoid sues for a truce with
Cyril the Sentimental Cynic: Yes, we're all
done for. Let's get the show on the road.

52

Moniza Alvi and **Peter Daniels** are the joint winners of The Poetry Business Competition 1991.

Moniza Alvi was born in Pakistan and grew up in Hertfordshire. She now lives in London, where she teaches at a girls' comprehensive school. For two years she was co-editor of *Poetry London Newsletter*.

Peter Daniels also lives in London, where he works as a librarian and indexer. He edited *Take Any Train: a book of gay men' s poetry* (Oscars Press 1990). He has recently spent some time in Minneapolis as guest editor of *The James White Review*.

Ackowledgements:
Moniza Alvi: *Agenda, London Magazine, London Review of Books, Nutshell, Poetry London Newsletter, Poetry Review, The Bound Spiral, The North, The Rialto, Transformation, Writng Women,* Cardiff Poetry Competition 1991.
Peter Daniels: *Gairfish, Orbis, Scratch, Breakfast in Bed* (Oscars Press), *Take Any Train* (Oscars Press), *Of Eros and of Dust* (Oscars Press), *The Crazy Jig* (Polygon), Kent & Sussex Competition Anthology 1991 (4th prize), National Poetry Competition 1990 Anthology.

The companion Anthology, *Greek Gifts*, is also published by Smith/ Doorstop Books, and is available from The Poetry Business.

For a full list of our publications (poetry books, cassettes, and *The North* magazine) and for details of the current Competition and our other activities, send an sae to The Poetry Business, 51 Byram Arcade, Westgate, Huddersfield HD1 1ND.